Chronicles of England, Scotland and Ireland

Raphael Holinshed

Contents

WILLIAM RUFUS, OR WILLIAM THE RED. 7

CHRONICLES OF ENGLAND, SCOTLAND AND IRELAND

BY

Raphael Holinshed

WILLIAM RUFUS, OR WILLIAM THE RED.

William, surnamed Rufus or William the Red, second sonne to William Conqueror, began his reigne ouer England the ninth of September, in the yeare 1087. about the 31. yeare of the emperour Henrie the fourth, and the 37. of Philip the first, king of France, Urbane the second then gouerning the see of Rome, and Malcolme Cammoir reigning in Scotland. [Note: Polydor. Sim. Dunel. Matth. Paris.] Immediatlie after his fathers deceasse, and before the solemnitie of the funerals were executed, he came ouer into England with no lesse speed than was possible, and following the counsell of Lanfranke archbishop of Canturburie (in whome he reposed all his trust) he sought to win the fauour of the Peers and Nobilitie of the realme by great and liberall gifts. For although there were but few of the homeborne states that bare rule in the land at this season; yet those that remained, and whome his father in extreme sort had wronged, he verie gentlie enterteined, promising them not onlie to continue their good lord and souereigne, but also to make more fauourable ordinances than his father had left behind him; and furthermore to restore the former lawes and liberties of the realme, which his said father had abolished. Thus by faire words and politic he obtained his purpose. [Note: Sim. Dunel. Marchar and Wilnot.] Howbeit soone after he forgat himselfe, and imprisoned Marchar and Wilnot, whom he had brought ouer with him from Normandie, being set at libertie by his father.

[Note: Lanfranke had fauoured him euen of a child. Matth. Paris. ***William Rufus is crowned the 26. of September.*** Polydor. His bountifull munificence.] The nobles at the first wished rather to haue had the elder brother duke Robert to haue gouerned them: howbeit by the aide onelie of the said Lanfranke, whose authoritie was of no small force amongst all the lords of the land, this William (according to his fathers assignation) was proclaimed and crowned at Westminster on the 26. of September (being Sundaie, the 6. kalends of October) and the 11. indiction, as the best writers doo report. After his coronation, to gratifie the people, he went to Winchester, where he found great treasure which his father had laid vp there for his owne vse: this he freelie spent in large gifts, and all kind of princelie largesse. He set verie manie prisoners at libertie, and did many other things to benefit the people, wherein the diligence and good aduice of Lanfranke did not a little preuaile. For he perceiued that there was in the king a variable mind, an vnstable nature, and a disposition to lightnesse and follie. Wherefore hee tooke oftentimes the more paines in persuading him not onelie to liberalitie (which is none of the least vertues in a prince) but also to vse a discreet and orderlie behauiour in all his dooings. Moreouer, he sticked not to put him in feare of an euill end, and troublesome regiment likelie to insue, if he did giue himselfe to vice and wilfulnesse, & neglect the charge thus by the prouidence of GOD committed to his hands. After this maner did the said prelat trauell with the king, whom we will leaue at this time as it were hearkening to his admonitions, and set foorth by the waie what his brother Robert did, whilest William Rufus his brother was occupied in such wise as you haue heard.

It happened that this Robert was abroad in Germanie, when king

William his father died (whither he went to raise a power, to the intent he might therby obteine the possession of Normandie, which he trusted to enioy in his fathers life time) where hearing newes of his death, he hasted straightwaies into Normandie, and there being ioyfullie receiued, was peaceablie proclaimed duke of that countrie, with great gladnesse and shouting of the people.

[Note: 1088.] After this, considering with himselfe how dishonorable a thing it was for him, that his yoonger brother should possesse the crowne of England, which of right (as he said) belonged vnto him, by reason of his age; he determined with all expedition to passe the seas with an armie, and recouer that into his hands, which his father had giuen from him, partlie (as it is thought) for his wilfulnesse and disobedience towards him, and partly also bicause he doubted that if he should leaue it vnto him, he would through his too much gentlenesse and facilitie, giue occasion to the English to resume strength, and therby to reuolt. Wherefore he iudged his yoonger brother the saied William (a man of a rougher nature) the meeter of the twaine for the gouernement.

As duke Robert was thus mooued by his owne desire to bereue his brother of the dominion of England, so he was not a little incensed thervnto by such of the English Nobilitie and Normans, as came dailie ouer vnto him out of the realme, complaining of the present state of the world, as those misliked of the whole maner of regiment vsed in the beginning of the reigne of his brother William. His vncle Odo also (then bishop of Baieux) furthered the matter all that he might. This Odo was at first in great estimation with his brother the Conqueror, and bare great rule vnder him, till at length for enuie that the archbishop Lanfranke was preferred before him, he conspired against him, who vnderstanding thereof, committed him foorthwith to prison, where he remained, till the said prince then lieng on his death-bed, released and restored him to his former libertie. When the king was dead, William Rufus tooke him backe into England, supposing no lesse but to haue had a speciall freend and a trustie counceller of him in all his affaires. But yer long after his comming thither, he fell againe into the same offense of ingratitude, wherof he became culpable in the Conquerors daies: for perceiuing that Lanfranke was so highlie esteemed with the king, that he could beare no rule, and partlie suspecting that Lanfranke had been cheefe causer of his former imprisonment, [Note: Odo the bishop of Baieux conspireth against his nephue William Rufus.] he conspired with the rest against his nephue, and therevpon wrote sundrie letters ouer vnto duke Robert, counselling him to come ouer with an armie in all hast, to take the rule vpon him, which by his practise should easilie be compassed.

Duke Robert being thus animated on all sides, and yet wanting suf-ficient monie to the furniture of this iournie, engaged a portion of his duchie of Normandie, as the countie of Constantine to his yoongest brother Henrie, for a great sum of gold, and therwith returned answer to the foresaid bishop, that he should prouide and looke for him vpon the south coast of England, at a certeine time appointed. [Note: The castell of Rochester.] Herevpon Odo fortified the castell of Rochester, & began to make sore wars against the kings friends in Kent: he procured others of the complices also to do the like in other parts of the realme; [Note: Simon Dun. Wil. Malm. The bishop of Constance taketh the town of Bath.] and first on the west part of England, where Geffrey bishop of Constans with his nephue Robert de Mowbray earle of Nor-thumberland setting foorth from Bristow, came toward Bath, which towne they tooke and sacked, and likewise Berkley, with a great part of Wiltshire, and brought the spoile and booties backe to Bristow, where they had a castell stronglie fortified for their more safetie. In like maner Roger de Bygod, departing from Norwich, with great forraies ouerrode and robbed all the countries about, and conueied such riches as he had gotten into the said citie. [Note: Hugh Grandmesnill. Hen. Hunt. Wil. Mal.] In like sort did Hugh de Grandmesnill at Leiceister, spoiling and wasting all the countries about him.

[Note: The earle of Shrewsburie.] The earle of Shrewsburie called Roger de Mountgomerie, with a power of Welshmen set foorth from Shrewsburie, and with him were William bishop of Durham the kings houshold chapline, Barnard of Newmerch, Roger Lacie, and Rafe Mortimer, (all Normans or Frenchmen) who ioyning their powers togither, inuaded the countrie, and with fire and sword did much hurt where they came, killing and taking a great number of people. [Note: Worcester assaulted.] Afterwards comming to Worcester, they assaulted the citie, ouerran the suburbs, & set the same on fire. But the citizens shutting fast the gates of their citie (though with the sudden comming of the enimies they were somewhat afraid) made valiant resistance; and conueieng their goods, their wiues, and their children into the castell, got them to the walles and places of defense, to repell and beat backe the enimies. [Note: Bishop Woolstan.] Among them in the towne was bishop Woolstan, whom the citizens would haue compelled to go into the castell for his surer safegard, but he refused it.

At length it chanced that the enimies (continuing the said siege) began to wax negligent, and ranged abroad in the countrie, little regarding watch and ward about their campe, wherevpon the English within the citie tooke this oportunitie, being mooued thereto with the comfortable exhortation of bishop Woolstan, and sailing foorth of the towne did set on their enimies with great fiercenes, whome they got at such aduantage, [Note: They slue fiue hundred, and chased the residue as

saith Simon Dunel.] that they slue and tooke that daie aboue fiue M.
men (as Henrie of Huntingdon recordeth.) For the English bearing a
continuall malice in their hearts against the French and Normans, did
now their best to be fullie reuenged of them, vpon so conuenient an occasion offered. Those that escaped by flight, hid themselues in the next
townes, making such shifts for their liues as the present necessitie could
minister.

[Note: The diligence of the archbishop Lanfranke.] Whilest the
realme was thus troubled on ech side, archbishop Lanfranke sendeth,
writeth, and admonisheth all the kings freends to make themselues
readie to defend their prince. And after he vnderstood that they were
assembled togither for that purpose, he counselleth the king to march
into the field with them speedilie, to represse his enimies. [Note: The
great curtesie shewed to the Englishmen by Wil. Rufus. Simon Dun.]
The king following his counsell, first appointed his nauie to scowre and
keepe the seas, and to withstand (if it were possible) the arriuall of his
brother by faire words. Also he reconcileth Roger de Mountgomerie
earle of Shrewsburie vnto him, and therewith maketh large promises
to the English, that he would out of hand giue and restore vnto them
such fauourable lawes as they would wish or desire. Moreouer he commanded all vniust imposts, tolles and tallages to be laid downe, and
granted free hunting in the woods, chases and forrests. All which grants
and promises he kept not long, though for the time he greatlie contented the people with such a shew of good meaning towards them.
[Note: Wil. Malm.] This doone, he goeth with a mightie armie into
Kent, where the sedition began, and first comming to the castell of Tun-
bridge, he compelled capteine Gilbert to yeeld vp the fortresse into his
hands. Then went he to Horne castell, where he heard saie Odo was
(but the report was vntrue, for he had betaken himselfe to the castell of

Pemsey) which when he had ouerthrowne, he hasted forth vnto Pemsey, and besieged the castell there a long season, which the bishop had stronglie fortified.

During this time, and about the fiftieth daie after the beginning of the siege, word was brought to the king, that his brother duke Robert was landed at Southampton, and minded with all possible speed to come to the succour of the bishop, and of other his freends, whom he and his power had not a little afflicted. [Note: H. Hunt. Simon Dun.] ¶ Here authors varie: for some report that duke Robert came not ouer himselfe the first at all, but sent a part of his armie, with a certeine number of ships, which encountring with the kings fleet, were discomfited. Others write that duke Robert hearing of the losse of his men, came after himselfe, and landed with a mightie armie as before, which is most likelie. [Note: Gemeticensis. Eustace earle of Bullongne.] And certeinlie (as Gemeticen. affirmeth) he might easilie as then haue recouered England from his brother, if he had not lingred the time, considering that Eustace earle of Bullongne, Odo bishop of Baieux, and the earle of Mortaigne, with other lords of Normandie that were passed to England, had alreadie taken Rochester, and diuers other castels in the prouince of Canturburie, keeping the same a certeine time, still looking that he should haue come ouer to their aid, which he deferred to doo, till they were constreined by siege and lacke of necessarie succor to returne into Normandie, leauing those places which they had won vnto the king, and that to their great dishonor. [Note: Simon Dun.] But howsoeuer it was, the king still continued the siege before Pemsey castell, till Odo (through want of victuals) was glad to submit himselfe, and promised to cause the castell of Rochester to be deliuered: but at his comming thither, they within the citie suffered him to enter, and streightwaies laid him fast in prison. Some iudge that it was doone vnder a colour by his owne consent.

There were in Rochester a sort of valiant gentlemen (the flower in maner of all Normandie) with Eustace earle of Bolongne, and manie gentlemen of Flanders, which were in mind to defend the place against the king: [Note: Rochester besieged by the king.] who hearing what was doone, came with his armie and besieged the citie of Rochester on ech side so sharpelie, that they within were glad to deliuer it vp into his hands. [Note: An. Reg. 2.] [Note: Polydor.] [Note: 1089.] Thus lost bishop Odo all his liuings and dignities in England, and so returned into Normandie, where vnder duke Robert he had the cheefe gouernement of the countrie committed vnto him.

After this he ouercame diuers of his enimies some by faire and some by fowle meanes. Notwithstanding this, there yet remained the bishop of Durham, one of the cheefe conspirators, who withdrew himselfe into the citie of Durham, there to lie in safetie, till he saw how the world would go: but being therein besieged by the king, who came thither personallie, he was at length forced to surrender the city, and yeeld himselfe: [Note: The bishop of Durham exiled.] wherevpon also he was exiled the land, with diuerse of his complices. But within two yeares after, he was called home againe, and restored to his church, wherein he liued not long, but died for sorrow, bicause he could not cleere himselfe of offense in the said rebellion, albeit that he laboured most earnestlie so to doo, that he might thereby haue atteined to the kings fauor againe.

[Note: Lanfranke archbishop of Canturburie departeth this life.] Whilest these things were thus in hand, the archbishop Lanfranke falleth sicke and dieth, in the 19. yeare after his first entring into the gouerment of the sea of Canturburie. This Lanfranke (as should seeme) was a wise, politike, and learned prelate, who whilest he liued, molli-fied the furious and cruell nature of king William Rufus, instructing him to forbeare such wild and outragious behauiours as his youthfulnesse was inclined vnto: and moreouer persuaded the English to obey the same king as their loiall prince, whereby they should occasion him to be their good lord and king, not vsing them rigorouslie as his father had doon. So that Lanfranke could not well haue beene spared in the time of the rebellion, without great danger of subuerting the state of the commonwealth. He builded two hospitals without the citie of Canturburie, for the releefe of poore people and strangers, the one of S. John, the other at Harbaldowne. He aduanced the church of Rochester from foure secular clerkes, to the number of fiftie moonkes: [Note: Matth. Westm. Paule abbat of S. Albons] he repaired Christes church in Canturburie, and the abbey of S. Albons, whereof he made one Paule that was his nephue abbat, which Paule gouerned that house by his vncles assistance greatlie to the aduancement thereof, as well in temporall as spirituall preferments, as it was then iudged. Likewise the said Lanfranke was verie fortunate in the gouernement of his church and see of Canturburie, recouering sundrie portions of lands and rents alienated from the same before his daies, insomuch that he restored to that see 25 manors. [Note: Eadmerus.] For amongst other, whereas Odo the bishop of Baieux, who also was earle of Kent, bearing great rule in England vnder his nephue king William the Conquerour, had vsurped diuerse possessions which belonged to the see of Canturburie, and had seized the franchises apperteining to the same Lanfranke, into his owne hands, by sute and earnest trauell he recouered the same, and being impleaded about that matter by the said Odo, he so defended his cause, that in the end (though with much adoo) he had his will, and so remained in quiet possession of his right after that so long as he liued, without any trouble or vexation concerning the said possessions and liberties.

Whereas also not onelie Walkhem the bishop of Winchester, but diuerse other bishops in England were in mind to haue displaced moonks out of their cathedrall churches, and to haue brought canons into their roomes, Lanfranke withstood them, and would tollerate no such dislocation: [Note: Lanfranke praised for holding with the moonks.] an act at that time so well liked, that he was highlie commended for the same. [Note: The king giuen to sensuall lust and couetousnesse.] After Lanfrankes death, the king began greatlie to forget himselfe in all his dealings, insomuch that he kept many concubines, and waxed verie cruell and inconstant in all his dooings, so that he became an heauie burthen vnto his people. For he was so much addicted to gather goods, that he considered not what perteined to the maiestie of a king, insomuch that nothing tending to his gaine, and the satisfieng of his appetite, was esteemed of him vnlawfull, sith he measured all things by the vncontrolled rule of his roialtie, and considered nothing what so high an office required. He kept the see of Canturburie foure yeares in his hands, to see who would giue most for it, in the meane time taking the profits thereof, and making the vttermost of the same that by any meanes could be deuised.

[Note: Matth. Paris.] The like he vsed when other benefices and abbeies were vacant, and furthermore that little which the prince spared, his officers and farmers, no lesse couetous than he, conuerted to their aduantage: so that what by the king, and what by his procurators, the church of England was now sore charged and fleeced of hir wealth. Diuerse of hir prelates in like maner were not a little offended, to see their mother so spoiled of hir treasure and liuelihood, insomuch that they practised a redresse: and to begin withall, complained of the king to pope Vrban: but he was so busied with other troubles of his owne neerer home, that he could haue no time to seeke meanes how to redresse enormities a far off, [Note: Wil. Malm. Matt. Paris.] whereby the lands and goods belonging to the church here in England were still wastfullie spent and consumed by the king and others, to whome he gaue or let them foorth to farme at his owne pleasure, and to his most commoditie.

But albeit the prince was of such a disposition by nature, yet there is one thing written of him which ought not to be forgotten, to admonish vs that there is no man of so euill an affection, but that sometime he dealeth vprightlie, though it be by hap or other extraordinarie motion. It chanced that an abbeie was void of an abbat, wherein were two moonkes verie couetous persons aboue the rest, and such as by scraping and gathering togither, were become verie rich, for such (saith Polydor) in those daies mounted to preferment. These two appointed to go togither to the court, ech hoping at their comming thither to find some meanes that he might be made abbat of that house. Being thus agreed, to the court they come, and there offer verie largelie to the king to obteine their sute: who perceiuing their greedie desires, and casting his eies about the chamber, espied by chance an other moonke (that came to beare them companie, being a more sober man, and simple after his outward appearance) whom he called vnto him, and asked what he would giue him to be made abbat of the foresaid abbeie. The moonke after a little pause, made answere, that he would giue nothing at all for anie such purpose, since he entred into that profession of meere zeale to despise riches & all worldlie pompe, to the end he might the more quietlie serue God in holinesse & puritie of conuersation. Saiest thou so, quoth the king, then art thou euen he that art worthie to gouerne this house: and streightwaie he bestowed the house vpon him, iustlie refusing the other two, to their open infamie and reproch.

[Note: Matt. Paris.] [Note: An. Reg. 3. 1090.] But to returne to our historie. After the expulsion of the bishop of Durham, and other of his adherents, the king passed ouer into Normandie, purposing to depriue his brother of that dukedome, and being arriued there, he besieged and tooke S. Ualerie, Albemarle, and diuerse other townes and castels, wherein he placed a number of his best souldiers, [Note: Simon Dun. Warres betwixt the king and his brother Robert.] the better to mainteine warre against his foresaid brother. Herevpon also the said Robert sent vnto the French king for aid, who came downe at his request with a noble armie, and besieged one of those castels which king William had latelie woone; howbeit by such meanes as king William made, in sending to the French king an huge summe of monie, he raised his siege shortlie & returned home againe. [Note: An. Reg. 4 1091.] [Note: Gemeticensis. *A peace concluded.* Simon Dun. Matth. West. Matt. Paris.] At length a peace was concluded betwixt king William and the duke his brother, but yet verie dishonorable to the said Robert: for it was accorded, that king William should reteine & still inioy the countie of Ewe, with Fescampe, the abbasie of mount S. Michell, Chereburg, and all those other places which he had woone & gotten out of his hands in this his late voiage. On the other side it was agreed, that king William should aid the duke to recouer all other places beyond the seas, which belonged to their father. Also, that such Normans as had lost anie of their lands & liuings in England, for taking part with the duke in the late rebellion, should be restored to the same. And furthermore, that whether soeuer of both should die first, the suruiuer should be his heire, and succeed in his dominions.

[Note: Gemeticensis.] This peace was concluded at Caen, and that by procurement of the French king, at what time king William was verie strong in the field neare vnto Ewe. After which conclusion, they vnited their powers, and besieged their yoongest brother Henrie in the castell of mount S. Michell, which (being situat in the confines of Normandie and Britaine) he had stronglie fortified not long before for feare of afterclaps. But when they had lien about it by the space of all the Lent season, and had made manie bickerings with his men, more to their losse than lucre, they raised their siege, and voluntarilie departed. [Note: Sim. Dunel.] Not long after this, king William depriued Edgar Etheling of his honor, which duke Robert had assigned vnto him, banishing him out of Normandie for euer.

Shortlie after also the aforesaid Henrie wan a strong towne called Damfront, and furnishing it at all points, he kept the same in his possession as long as he liued, mauger both his brethren. Thus the war waxed hot betweene those three, howbeit suddenlie (I wot not vpon what occasion) this Henrie was reconciled with king William and his brother Robert, so that all debates being quieted on euerie side, they were made friends and welwillers. King William also returned into England, hauing his brother Robert in his companie, all men reioising at their pacification and amitie, which happened in the yeare 1091, and fourth of the reigne of the king.

Toward the end whereof, and vpon the fift daie of October, a maruellous sore tempest fell in sundrie parts of England, but especiallie in the towne of Winchcombe, where (by force of thunder and lightning) a part of the steeple of the church was throwne downe, and the crucifix with the image of Marie standing vnder the rood-loft, was likewise ouerthrowne, broken, and shattered in peeces; then folowed a foule, a noisome, and a most horrible stinke in the church. [Note: A mightie wind.] On the 17. daie of the same moneth much harme was doone in London with an outragious wind, the violence whereof ouerturned and rent in peeces aboue fiue hundred houses, at which time and tempest the roofe of S. Marie bowe church in cheape was also ouerthrowne, wherewith two men were slaine. [Note: An. Reg. 5. 1092.] Moreouer, at Salisburie much hurt was doone with the like wind and thunder, for the top of the steeple and manie buildings besides were sore shaken and cast downe. But now we will speake somewhat of the doings of Scotland, as occasion moueth. [Note: The scots inuade England.] Whilest (as yee haue heard) variance depended betweene king William and his brother duke Robert, the Scotish king Malcolme made sore wars vpon the inhabitants of Northumberland, carrieng great booties and preies out of that countrie, which he inuaded euen to Chester in the street. Wherefore king William, soone after his returne, gathered his power togither, and sped him northwards. But king Malcolme hearing of his puissance & great strength sent to him for peace, which was granted in the end.

[Note: Wil. Malm. Sim. Dun.] Some writers affirme, that king William prepared a great armie both by sea and land against Malcolme; and that his nauie being abroad on the seas, was lost by tempest, and the most part of his ships drowned; that the armie by land entring into Scotland, suffered manie damages through want of vittels, and so recoiled: finallie, that duke Robert lieng on the borders with an armie in his brothers name (wherby it should appeare that the king himselfe was not there) by the helpe and furtherance of Edgar Etheling, who then serued K. Malcolme in his wars, concluded a peace betwixt his brother and the said Malcolme, vpon certeine articles, by vertue wherof certeine places in Northumberland were restored vnto Malcolme, which he had held in William Conquerours daies. Some other write in like maner, that king Malcolme did homage to king William and duke Robert that brought the said Edgar Etheling into the fauour of the king.

Howsoeuer the truth of the storie dooth stand in this behalfe, certeine it is, that the king returned out of Northumberland into the west parts of the realme, reteining still with him duke Robert, who looked dailie when he should performe such couenants as were concluded vpon betwixt them in their late reconciliation. But when he saw that the king meant nothing lesse than to stand to those articles, and how he did onlie protract and delaie the time for some other secret purpose, he returned into Normandie in great displeasure, and tooke with him the said Edgar Etheling, of whom he alwaies made verie great account. [Note: The repairing and new peopling of Carleil.] Soone after king William returned into the north parts, and (as it chanced) he staied a few daies about Carleil, where being delited with the situation of the towne (which had beene destroied by the Danes two hundred yeares before) he set workemen to repaire the same (meaning to vse it in steed of a bulworke against the Scots on those west borders) which when he had fensed with walles, and builded a castell in the most conuenient place thereof, he caused churches and houses to be erected for the benefit of such people as he had determined to bring vnto the same. This being doone, he placed a colonie of southren men there with their wiues and children and gaue large priuileges vnto the towne, which they inioy at this daie.

[Note: Matth. West.] ¶ Here haue I thought good to aduertise you of an error in Matth. West. crept in either through misplacing the matter by means of some exemplifier, either else by the authors mistaking his account of yeares, as 1072. for 1092. referring the repairing of Carleil vnto William Conquerour, at what time he made a iournie against the Scots in the said yeare 1072. And yet not thus contented; to bewraie the error more manifestlie, he affirmeth that the king exchanged the earledome of Chester with Rafe or Ranulfe de Micenis, alias Meschines, for the earledome of Carleil, which the said Meschines held before, and had begunne there to build and fortifie that towne: whereas it is certeine that Ranulfe de Meschines came to enioy the earledome of

Chester by way of inheritance, as after shall appeare. For better proofe whereof ye shall vnderstand, that we find by ancient records, how one Hugh Lou or Lupus enioied the earledome of Chester all the daies of the Conqueror, and long after, which Hugh was sonne to Richard earle of Auranges and the countesse Emma daughter of a noble man in Normandie named Herlowin, who maried Arlet the daughter of a burgesse in Falois, and mother to William Conquerour. So that the said Hugh, being sisters sonne to the Conqueror, receiued by gift at his hands the earledome of Chester, to hold of him as freelie by right of the sword, as he held the realme of England in title of his crowne. For these be the words: "Tenendum sibi & haeredibus ita libere ad gladium, sicut ipse (Rex) totam tenebat Angliam ad coronam."

Earle Hugh then established in possession of this earledome, with most large priuileges and freedoms, for the better gouernement thereof, ordeined vnder him foure barons; [Note: Foure barons. Nigell or Neal. Piers Malbanke. * Eustace whose surname we find not. Warren Vernon.] namelie, his cousine Nigell or Neal baron of Halton, sir Piers Malbanke baron of Nauntwich, sir Eustace * baron of Mawpasse, and sir Warren Uernon baron of Shipbrooke. Nigell held his baronie of Halton by seruice, to lead the Uauntgard of the earles armie when he should make anie iournie into Wales; so as he should be the foremost in marching into the enimies countrie, and the last in comming backe: he was also conestable and Marshall of Chester. [Note: The Lacies.] From this Nigell or Neal, the Lacies that were earles of Lincolne had their originall. When earle Hugh had gouerned the earledome of Chester the terme of 40. yeares, he departed this life, in the yeare 1107. He had issue by his wife Armetrida, Richard the second earle of Chester after the conquest; Robert, abbat of Saint Edmundsburie: and Otnell, tutor to the children of king Henrie the first. [Note: Iohn Bohun.] Moreouer, the said earle

Hugh had a sister named Margaret, that was maried to John Bohun, who had issue by hir, Ranulfe Bohun, otherwise called Meschines, which Ranulfe by that meanes came to enioy the earledome of Chester in right of his mother (after that earle Richard was drowned in the sea) and not by exchange for the earledome of Carleil, as by this which we haue alreadie recited may sufficientlie be prooued.

[Note: An. Reg. 6.] Now to returne where we left. After that king William Rufus had giuen order for the building, fortifieng, and peopling of Carleil, he returned southwards, and came to Glocester, where he fell into a greeuous and dangerous sicknesse; [Note: 1093.] so that he was in despaire and doubt of his life: [Note: Simon Dun. Hen. Hunt. Matth. Paris. *The king being sicke promiseth amendment of life.* Polydor. Eadmerus.] wherefore he repented him of his former misdeeds, and promised (if he escaped that dangerous sicknesse) to amend and become a new man. But when he had his health, that promise was quickelie broken, for his dooings which were so bad and wicked before his sicknesse, being compared with those which followed after his recouerie, might haue beene reputed good and sufferable.

[Note: Anselme elected archbishop of Canturburie.] Moreouer, whereas he reteined and kept in his hands the bishoprike of Canturburie the space of foure yeares, he now bestowed it vpon Anselme, who was before abbat of Bechellouin in Normandie; and for certeine abbeis which he had held long time in his possession, he ordeined abbats: by meane wherof all men (but especiallie the spiritualtie) began to conceiue a verie good opinion of him. [Note: Eadmerus.] The yere wherein Anselme was thus elected, was from the birth of our Sauiour 1093. on the sixt of March, being the first sundaie in Lent (as Eadmerus recordeth.) [Note: Matth. Paris. Polydor. Robert Bluet L. Chancelor elected bishop of Lincolne.] Furthermore he gaue the see of Lincolne (being

void by the death of Bishop Remigius) to his councellour Robert Bluet; but afterward repenting himselfe of such liberalitie, in that he had
not kept it longer in his hands towards the inriching of his coffers, he
deuised a shift how to wipe the bishops nose of some of his gold, which
he performed after this maner. He caused the bishop to be sued, quarel-
inglie charging him that he had wrongfullie vsurped certeine possessions, togither with the citie of Lincolne, which appertained to the see
of Yorke. [Note: Hen. Hunt.] Which although it was but a forged cauil-
lation, and a shamefull vntruth; yet could not the bishop be deliuered
out of that trouble, till he had paid to the king fiue thousand pounds.
And as he dealt with the spiritualtie, so he caused diuerse of the Nobilitie to be put to greeuous fines, for transgressing of his lawes, though
the fault were neuer so little. He also caused the archbishop Anselme to
paie him a great summe of monie, vnder colour of a contribution which
was due in Lanfrankes daies, though it was certeinlie knowne that Lanfranke had paied it. Thus grew king William from time to time more
sharpe and rigorous to his subiects, so that whosoeuer came within the
danger of the laws, was sure to be condemned; and such as would plaie
the promooters and giue informations against any man for transgressing
the lawes, were highlie rewarded.

In this sixt yeare there chanced such an excessiue raine, and such
high flouds, the riuers ouerflowing the low grounds that lay neere vnto
them, as the like had not beene seene of many yeares before; and afterwards insued a sudden frost, whereby the great streames were congeled
in such sort, that at their dissoluing or thawing, manie bridges both of
wood and stone were borne downe, and diuerse water-milles rent vp
and caried awaie.

[Note: Polydor.] Furthermore king William perceiuing that by
his cruell and couetous gouernment, sundrie of his subiects did dailie

steale out of the realme, [Note: A proclamation that none should depart the realme.] to liue in forreine countries, he published a proclamation, charging that no man should depart the realme without his licence and safe-conduct. Hereof it is thought, that the custome rose of forbidding passage out of the realme, which oftentimes is vsed as a law, when occasion serueth. Soone after, he went against the Welshmen, whom he vanquished in battell neere to Brecknocke, and slue Rees their king, who had doone much hurt within the English borders, when he was their incamped. [Note: Ran. Higd. Rees king of Wales slaine.] This Rise or Rees was the last king that reigned ouer the Welshmen, as authors affirme: for afterwards, though they oftentimes rebelled, yet the kings of England were reputed and taken as supreme gouernors of that part of the Iland. [Note: Wil. Thorne.] Moreouer, to haue the countrie the better in quiet, he did cut downe their woods, and builded manie castels and piles in places conuenient, by meanes whereof they were somewhat tamed, and trained in due time to obedience, though not at the first, nor in the daies of sundrie of his successors.

[Note: Malcolme king of Scots commeth to Glocester. Wil. Malm. Polydor.] Hauing thus finished his iournie into Wales, Malcolme king of Scotland came vnto Glocester to see the king, and to common with him of sundrie matters touching the peace betwixt both the realms, as he returned homewards: but bicause king William disdained to enterteine him in such pompous maner as he expected and made account of; [Note: K. Malcolme inuadeth England.] and forsomuch as he did not at the verie first admit him to his presence, the said Malcolme returned into Scotland in great displeasure, and immediatelie raising a power, entred into England, destroieng the country vnto Alnewike castell, where he was so enuironed with an ambushment laid by Robert earle of Northumberland, that he and his eldest sonne Edward were slaine. At which mishap his whole host being vtterlie discomfited, fled out of the field with the losse of manie, whereof some were slaine, and some taken by pursute. [Note: Simon Dun.] Thus came king Malcolme to his end (by the iust prouidence of God) in that prouince which he had wasted and spoiled at fiue seuerall times, as first in the daies of king Edward, when earle Tostie was gone to Rome; the second time, in the daies of William Conquerour, when he spoiled Cleueland; thirdlie, in the same Conquerours daies, whilest bishop Walkher possessed the see of Durham, at what time all the countrie was spoiled and forraied, euen to the riuer of Tine; fourthlie, about the fourth or fift yeare of the reigne of this William Rufus, at which time he entered the land as farre as Chester in the street, whilest king William was in Normandie; the fift time was now, when he lost his life on saint Brices day, by the hands of a verie valiant knight named Morkell. King Malcolme being thus surprised by death, his bodie was buried at Tinmouth (as in the Scotish histories more plainelie appeareth) where also ye may find, how the sonnes of king Malcolme were aided by king William Rufus to obteine the crowne of Scotland, wherevnto they were interessed; whereas otherwise by the force and practise of their vncle Donald they had beene kept from the scepter and crowne of the kingdome.

[Note: Ran. Higd.] [Note: An. Reg. 7. 1094] This yeare England and Normandie were sore vexed with mortalitie both of men and beasts, insomuch that tillage of the ground was laid aside in manie places, by reason whereof there folowed great dearth & famine. [Note: Ran. Higd. Wil. Malm. Simon Dun. **Death & murren of cattell. Strange woonders.** Matth. Paris. Polydor. Simon Dun.] Manie grizelie and hideous sights were seene also in England, as hosts of men fighting in the aire, flashes of fier, stars falling from heauen, and such like strange wonders. About this time new occasions of breach of amitie grew betwixt the king and his brother Robert, who accused him of periurie, for not obseruing the articles of the last peace concluded betwixt them: wherefore he purposed to saile ouer into Normandie, and so came vnto Hastings, about the first of Februarie, where he soiourned for a time, and caused the church of Battell abbeie to be dedicated in the honour of S. Martin. He depriued Herbert bishop of Thetford of his bishops staffe, because he meant to haue stolen awaie secretlie to Rome, and there to haue purchased absolution of pope Urban for his bishoprike, which he had bought of the king for himselfe; and likewise for the abbasie of Winchester, which he had purchased for his father, paieng for them both a thousand pounds.

[Note: King William passeth ouer into Normandie.] After this, about midlent he passed ouer into Normandie with an armie, purposing to trie the matter with his brother in plaine battell, that thereby he might rather grow to some certeine point of losse or lucre, than to stand ouer vpon vncerteinties, whether to haue peace or war, that he must be constreined to be at all times in a readinesse to defend himselfe. [Note: Wars betwixt the king and his brother.] But after he was come into Normandie, & had forraied part of the countrie once or twice, he fell to a parle with his brother duke Robert, & in the end condescended to put the matter in compromise to the arbitrement of certeine graue persons, whose iudgement the king reiected, bicause they gaue not sentence on his side. [Note: Matth. West.] Herevpon both parts prepared for war afresh, insomuch that the king perceiuing how his brother was aided by the French king, and that his power was too weake to withstand them both, he sent his commission into England for the leuieng of 20. thousand men, commanding that they should be sent ouer vnto him into Normandie by a daie, which was diligentlie performed. But as they were come togither about Hastings, readie to enter a shipboord, immediatlie commeth the kings lieutenant with a countermand, and signifieth to them, that the king minding to fauour and spare them for that iournie, would that euery of them should giue him 10. shillings (as Matt. Paris hath, or 20. shillings as others haue) towards the charges of the war, and therevpon depart home with a sufficient safeconduct; which the most part were better content to doo, than to commit themselues to the fortune of the sea, and bloudie successe of the wars in Normandie. [Note: Polydor.] In deed king William changing his mind, was now determined to end the matter with monie, and not with the sword, as it afterward appeered; for by bribing of king Philip, in whom duke Robert had reposed his whole trust, [Note: A peace concluded betwixt the king and his brother Robert.] he concluded peace vpon such articles and conditions as he himselfe required.

[Note: Hen. Hunt. Simon Dun. The Welshmen inuade England.] Hauing dispatched his businesse in Normandie, he returned into England, where he happened to meet with new and more dangerous wars: for the Welshmen hearing of the variance betwixt the brethren, after their accustomed maner begin to inuade the English marshes, taking booties of cattell, destroieng the countries, killing and spoiling many of the kings subiects, both English and Normans. [Note: The castell of Mountgomerie won by the Welshmen.] After this (waxing proud of their good successe) they besieged the castell of Mountgomerie, where though the garison made stout resistance for a time, yet in the end the enimie finding shift to ouerthrow the walles, entred perforce, and slue all that they found within. [Note: An. Reg. 8. 1095.] Wherewith though king William was offended when he heard of it, yet could he not remedie the matter as then, being troubled with a conspiracie newlie kindled against him by Robert earle of Northumberland, [Note: Robert earle of Northumberland refuseth to come to the king.] who vpon displeasure conceiued against him (bicause he was not rewarded nor thanked at his hands for his good seruice shewed in the killing of Malcolme king of Scotland) refused to come vnto him being sent for by letters, and herewith began to practise with certeine other Noble men of that countrie, how to depose king William. But yer he could bring anie peece of his purpose to passe, the king hauing aduertisement of his attempts, [Note: Matth. Paris.] first appointed his brother the lord Henrie to go thither with an armie, and foorthwith foloweth himselfe; and comming to Newcastell, where the most part of his complices were assembled, he surprised them yer they could haue time to prouide for their safetie. That doone, he went to Tinmouth, and in the castell tooke the earles brother there, and after came to Banbourgh castell, which the said earle with his wife and children did hold for their better safegard and defense.

[Note: Hen. Hunt.] Some authors write, that when the king perceiued it would be hard for him to win Banbourgh castell (by reason of the great strength thereof) without famine, [Note: Maluoisin a fortresse built against Banbourgh.] he builded vp an other castell or bastilion fast by it, calling the same Maluoisin, wherein he placed a great power of men, by whose meanes at length the earle was so narrowlie driuen, that when he sought to haue escaped by night, he was espied, [Note: Polydor.] and therewith pursued so closelie by the kings souldiers, that he was forced to take sanctuarie within the church of S. Oswins at Tinmouth, from whence he was quicklie taken, and brought as prisoner to the kings presence. Notwithstanding, those that remained within the castell vpon trust of the strength of that place, would not yeeld by anie meanes; but stood still to their tackling: wherevpon the king caused the earle their maister to be brought foorth before the gates, and threatened that he should haue his eies put out, if they within did not streightwaies giue vp the hold into his hands. [Note: Banbourgh yeelded to the king.]

Here vpon it came to passe, that the castell was yeelded, and those that kept it were diuerslie punished, some by banishment, some by loosing their eares, & diuerse by the losse of their hands, in example to others. The earle himselfe was conueied to Windsor castell, and there committed to prison.

[Note: Simon Dun. The earle of Ewe.] Some write that the meaning of the earle and his complices (amongst whom was William earle of Ewe, who renouncing his allegiance to Robert duke of Normandie, was become the kings man) was to haue displaced the king from his roiall throne, and to haue set vp his sonne William de Albemarle, whom he had begotten of his concubine. But whatsoeuer their purpose was, after that the king had quieted his countrie in the north parts, [Note: Matth. Paris.] he bent all his force against the Welshmen, who the yeare before had destroied and ouerthrowne the castell of Moungomerie, and slaine the Normans that laie there in garison to defend it, whereat he was verie much offended, [Note: King William inuadeth Wales.] & therefore entering into Wales, he began to spoile and wast the countrie. For he saw that the Welshmen would not ioine in battell with him in the plaine field, but kept themselues still aloofe within the woods and marishes, and aloft vpon mountaines: albeit oftentimes when they saw aduantage, they would come foorth, and taking the Englishmen and Normans at vnawares, kill manie, and wound no small numbers, he still pursued them by hils and dales, though more to the losse of his owne people than the hurt of the Welshmen, who easilie eschewed the danger of battell, and still at the straites and combersome passages distressed manie of their enimies: whereby the king at length perceiuing that he could not preuaile against them, ceassed further to follow on with his purposed voiage, and therewith returned home, not without some note of dishonor.[Note: The king returneth out of Wales with dishonour. Eadmerus. Murcherdach king of Ireland.]

About the same time Murcherdach king of Ireland, with the clergie and people of the citie of Dublin, elected one Samuell a moonke of S. Albons, an Irish man borne, to the gouernement of the church and bishops see of Dublin, and (according to the ancient custome) presented him by sufficient letters of testimonie vnto Anselme archbishop of Canturburie, to be consecrated of him, who (according to their request) did so, and receiued from him a promise of his canonicall subiection, after the old vsuall maner, hauing foure bishops (suffragans to the see of Canturburie) ministring to him at that consecration.

[Note: The councell of Clermount.] In like maner, pope Urban calling a councell at Clermont in Auuergne, exhorted the christian princes so earnestlie to make a iourneie into the holie land, [Note: The iournie into the holie land.] for the recouerie thereof out of the Saracens hands, that the said great and generall iournie was concluded vpon to be taken in hand; [Note: Godfray de Bullion.] wherein manie Noble men of christendome went vnder the leading of Godfray of Bullion, and others, as in the chronicles of France, of Germanie, and of the holie land dooth more plainlie appeare. There went also among other diuers Noble men foorth of this relme of England, speciallie that worthilie bare the surname of Beauchampe. [Note: An. Reg. 9. 1096.] Robert duke of Normandie minding also to go the same iournie, and wanting monie to furnish and set foorth himselfe, morgaged his duchie of Normandie to his brother king William, for the summe of ten thousand pounds. [Note: Hen. Hunt. Will. Thorne. Simon Dun. A subsidie.] About this time another occasion was offered vnto king William, to laie a new paiment vpon his subiects, so greeuous and intolerable, as well to the spiritualtie as the temporaltie, that diuerse bishops and abbats, who had alreadie made away some of their chalices and church iewels to paie the king, made now plaine answer that they were not able to helpe him with any more. Unto whom on the other side (as the report went) the king said againe; "Haue you not (I beseech you) coffins of gold and siluer full of dead mens bones:" Meaning the shrines wherein the re- likes of saints were inclosed. Which (as his words seemed to import) he would haue had them conuert into monie, therewith to helpe him in that need, iudging it no sacrilege, though manie did otherwise esteeme it, considering (as he pretended) that it was gathered for so godlie an vse, as to mainteine warres against Infidels and enimies of Christ.

[Note: Eadmerus.] The archbishop Anselme tooke the worth of two hundred markes of siluer of the iewels that belonged to the church of Canturburie (the greater part of the couent of moonks winking thereat) towards the making vp of such paiment as he was constreined to make vnto the king towards his aid at that time. But bicause he would not leaue this for an example to be followed of his successours, he granted to the church of Canturburie the profits and reuenues of his manour of Petteham, vnto the vse of the same church for the terme of seauen yeares, which amounted to the summe of thirtie pounds yearelie in those daies.

[Note: Polydor.] Thus king William seeking rather to spoile the realme of England, than to preserue the roiall state thereof, after he had gotten togither a great masse of monie, sailed ouer into Normandie, and there deliuering vnto the duke the ten thousand pounds aforesaid, was put in possession of the duchie, to enioy the same, and the profits rising thereof, till the said ten thousand pounds were paid him againe: [Note: The duchie of Normandie morgaged to king William. Eadmerus.] or (as some write) it was couenanted that in recompense thereof, the king should enioy the profits for terme onelie of three yeares, and then to restore it without any further interest or commoditie. [Note: Polydor.]

This doone, he returned againe into England.

Now duke Robert setteth forward on his iornie, in companie of other Noble men, towards the holie land. In which voiage his valorous hart at all assaies (when any seruice should be shewed) was most manifestlie perceiued, to his high fame and renowme among the princes and nobilitie there and then assembled.

[Note: An. Reg. 10. 1097.] [Note: Eadmerus. Waterford in Ireland made a bishoprike. The archbishop of Canturburie primate of Ireland.] About the same time, the citizens of Waterford in Ireland, perceiuing that by reason of the great multitude of people in that citie, it was necessarie for them to haue a bishop; obteined licence of their king and rulers to erect in their citie a bishops see, and besought them that it might please them to write vnto Anselme the archbishop of Canturburie their primate, to haue his consent therein, so as it might stand with his pleasure to institute and ordeine such a one bishop, to haue gouernement of their church, as they should name, knowing him to be a man of such learning, knowledge, discretion and worthines as were fit for the roome. [Note: Murcherdach K. of Ireland.] Herevpon were letters sent by messengers from Murcherdach king of Ireland vnto Anselme, informing him of the whole matter: wherein one Malchus was commended and presented vnto him to be admitted and consecrated, if he thought good. These letters were subscribed with the hands, not onelie of king Murcherdach, but also of his brother duke Dermeth, bishop Dufnald, Idiman bishop of Methe, Samuell bishop of Dublin, Ferdomnachus bishop of Laginia or Leinister, and many others both of the spiritualtie and temporaltie.

Anselme considering their request to be iust and necessarie, granted to fulfill their desires, and so vpon examination had of the man, and taking of him his oth of obedience, according to the maner, he consecrated the same Malchus, and so ordeined him to rule the church of Waterford as bishop. [Note: Malchus consecrated bishop of Waterford.] This was doone at Canturburie the 28. day of October, Rafe bishop of Chichester, and Gundulfe bishop of Rochester helping Anselme in the consecration as ministers vnto him in that behalfe. The said Malchus was a monke, and sometime vnder Walkhelme bishop of Winchester.

[Note: The king eftsoones inuadeth the Welshmen. Polydor.] But to the purpose, king William after his returne into England, remembring what damage he had susteined two yeeres before at the hands of the Welshmen, determined eftsoones to inuade their countrie, and therefore doubling his power, commeth into the marshes, pitcheth his field, and consulteth with his capteines what order he were best to vse in that his enterprise, for the taming of his enimies. The Welshmen hearing of the kings approch, and that his armie was farre greater than the last which he brought into their countrie, fell to their woonted policie, [Note: The Welshmen withdraw into the woods. H. Hunt.] and got them into the woods, there to lie in wait, trusting more to the aduantage of starting holes, than to their owne force & puissance.

When the king vnderstood their practise, he set armed men in diuers places, and builded towers and fortifications to defend him and his, bicause he durst not assaie to enter into wild and wast grounds where he had beene hindred and damnified before that time, hoping by this meanes in stopping vp the waies and passages of the countrie, to bring the rebels to more subiection. But when this policie was found by proofe to wearie the kings souldiors rather than to hurt the enimies, which straieng vp and downe in the woods intrapped oftentimes the Normans and English, in taking them at aduantage, the king without bringing his purpose to any good effect, departed home into England. [Note: Simon Dun. R. Houed.] After this he sent Edgar Etheling with an armie into Scotland, that he might place his coosine Edgar the sonne of king Malcolme in the gouernement of that kingdome, and expell his vncle Duffnald, who had vsurped the same.

[Note: An. Reg. 11. 1098.] King William, being still inflamed with ire, for that he could not haue his will, determined with continuall warres to wearie the rebellious stomachs of the Welshmen: and therefore was fixed first to set vpon them of Anglesey, which being an Ile enuironed with the sea, was euer a refuge for them when they were sharpelie pursued. [Note: Matth. Paris.] This enterprise was cheeflie committed vnto Hugh earle of Shrewsburie and Arundell, and to Hugh earle of Chester, who at their first comming wan the Ile, and tempered the victorie with great crueltie and bloudshed, putting out the eies of some, cutting off the noses, the armes, or hands of others, and some also they gelded. [Note: Gyral. Cam.] Moreouer (as authors write) the said earle of Shrewesburie made a kenell of the church of Saint Fridancus, laieng his hounds within it for the night time, but in the morning he found them all raging wood. How true so euer this report is I wote not, but shortlie after they had executed (in maner as before is said) such strange kinds of crueltie in that Ile, it chanced that a nauie of rouers came thither from the Iles of Orkney, whose cheefe admirall was named Magnus, who incountring with the said earle of Shrewesburie, [Note: Hugh earle of Shrewsburie slaine.] shot him into the eie with an arrow, which part of his body remained bare and vnarmed, so that by & by he fell downe dead out of his ship into the sea. When Magnus beheld this, he said scornefullie in the Danish toong, Leit loupe, that is; Let him leape now: the English neuerthelesse had the victorie at that time (as some write) and ouercame their enimies with great slaughter and bloudshed. [Note: Fab. ex Guido de Columna.] Not long after, the earle of Chester going ouer to Wales, with long and continual warres tired and tamed the wild Welshmen, who for a good while after durst not shew their faces.

[Note: An. Reg. 12. 1099.] The king being thus at quiet and without warre in all places, began now to set his mind on building, and first caused new walles to be made about the tower of London, and also laid the foundation, of Westminster hall, which though it be a verie large and roomthie place, yet after it was finished at his returne out of Normandie, he came to view it, held his court therein with great pompe and honor. [Note: Fabian. Ran. Higd. Matth. Paris.] He repented that he had made it no larger, saieng; it was too little by the halfe, and therefore determined to haue made a new, and that this other should haue serued but for a dining chamber. A diligent searcher (saith Matthew Paris) might yet find out the foundation of the hall, which he had purposed to build, stretching from the Thames side vnto the common street. But though those his buildings were great ornaments to the realme, yet bicause he tooke vp monie by extortion of his subiects towards the charges of the same, he was euill spoken of; [Note: Polydor.] the report being spred, that he should take them in hand but onelie vnder a colour to spoile his subiects, in gathering a farre greater summe than the expenses of them did amount vnto. [Note: The king goeth ouer into Normandie.] About the same time that king William beganne these buildings, he went ouer into Normandie, to vnderstand in what state that countrie stood.

[Note: Finchamsteed. Ran. Higd. Hen. Hunt. Matth. West. Wil. Malm.] About the same time also, or rather two yeere before; to wit 1097. neere to Abington, at a towne called Finchamsteed in Berkshire, a well or fountaine flowed with bloud, in maner as before it vsed to flow with water, and this continued for the space of three daies, or (as William Malmes. saith) fifteene daies togither.

After the king had dispatched his businesse in Normandie, & was returned into England (as he was making prouision to ride foorth on hunting) a messenger came suddenlie vnto him, bringing word, that the citie of Mans was besieged, and like to be surprised. [Note: Hen. Hunt. Matth. Paris.] The king was then at dinner, meaning first to make an end thereof, and after to take aduice in that matter: but being reprooued by the messenger, for that to the great danger of his subiects which were besieged he passed not to make delaies, rather than to go and succour them with all speed, he taketh the mans blunt speech in so good part, that he called straightwaie for masons to breake downe the wall, to the end he might passe through the next way, and not be driuen to step so farre out of his path, as to go foorth by the doores: and so without any long aduisement taken in the cause, he rode straightwaie to the sea, sending his lords a commandement to follow; [Note: Wil. Malm.] who when they came in his presence, counselled him to staie till his people were assembled. Howbeit he would not giue eare to their aduice in that point, but said; Such as loue me, I know well will follow me, and so went a shipboord, setting apart all doubts of perils; and yet was the weather verie darke, rough and cloudie, insomuch that the maister of the ship was afraid, and willed him to tarrie till the wind did settle in some quiet quarter: [Note: The saieng of king William Rufus.] but hee commanded to hoise vp sailes, and to make all speed that could be for life, incouraging the shipmaster with these words, "that he neuer heard as yet of anie king that was drowned."

Thus passing the seas, he landed in Normandie, where he gathered his power, and made towards Mans. When those which held the siege before the citie, heard of his approch, they brake vp their campe and departed thence: [Note: Mans deliuered from an asseege.] howbeit, the capteine named Helias, that pretended by title and right to be earle of

Mans, was taken by a traine; and brought before the king, who iested at him, as though he had beene but a foole and a coward. [Note: Helias.] Wherevpon, the said Helias kindled in wrath, boldlie said vnto him; "Whereas thou hast taken me prisoner, it was by meere chance, and not by thy manhood: but if I were at libertie againe, I would so vse the matter with thee, that thou shouldest not thinke I were a man so lightlie to be laughed at." "No should (saith the king); Well then I giue thee thy libertie, and go thy waies, doo euen the worst that lieth in thy power against me, for I care not a button for thee." Helias being, thus set at libertie, did nothing after (to make anie account of) against the king, but rather kept himselfe quiet. [Note: Hen. Hunt. Polydor.] Howbeit some write, that he was not taken at all, but escaped by flight. To proceed king William being returned into England, and puffed vp with pride of his victories, and now seeing himselfe fullie deliuered from all troubles of warre, began after his old manner to spoile and wast the countrie by vnreasonable exactions, tributes and paiments.

[Note: Variance betwixt the king and the archbishop Anselme.] Herevpon fell a great controuersie betweene Anselme and the king, who pretended a reproch of cruell surcharging of his commons with subsidies, lones, and vnreasonable fines: but the cheefe cause was, for that he might not call his synods, nor correct the bishops, but all to be doone as the king would. The king also chalenged the inuestiture of prelates, and indeed sore taxed both the spiritualtie and temporaltie, spending the monie vpon the reparations and buildings of the Tower, & Westminster hall, as is before remembred. Besides this, his seruants spoiled the English of their goods by indirect meanes: but especiallie one Rafe sometime chaplaine vnto William the Conquerour, & at this time the kings proctor and collector of his taskes and subsidies was so malicious & couetous, that in steed of two taskes, he would leuie

three, pilling the rich, and powling the poore, so that manie through
his cruell dealing were oftentimes made to forfeit their lands for small
offenses: and by his meanes also diuerse bishoprikes were bought and
sold as other kinds of merchandizes, whereby he was in singular fauour
with the king. [Note: The clergie out of order.] The clergie also
were vsed verie streightlie, and (as I suppose) not without good cause;
for suerlie in those daies it was far out of order, not onelie in couetous
practises, but in all kinds of worldlie pompe and vanitie: for they had
vp bushed and braided perukes, long side garments verie gorgeous, gilt
girdels, gilt spurs, with manie other vnseemelie disorders in attire. To
be short, the contention grew so hot betwixt the king and Anselme,
who would also haue corrected such vices in the clergie (as some write)
[Note: Matth. Paris.] that in the end the archbishop was quite cast out
of fauour. [Note: A thousand markes demanded of Anselme.] There are
which alledge the verie first and originall occasion of their falling out
to be, for that the archbishop denied to paie a thousand marks of siluer
at his request; in consideration of the great beneuolence shewed in pre-
ferring him to his see, whereas the archbishop iudged the offense of
simonie, to rest as well in giuing after his promotion receiued, as if he
had bribed him aforehand, and therefore refused to make anie such paiment: [Note: Eadmerus.] but yet (as Eadmerus writeth) he offered him
fiue hundred pounds of siluer, which would not be receiued, for the king
was informed by some of his councell, that the archbishop (in consideration of his bountious liberalitie extended towards him) ought rather
to giue him two thousand pounds, than fiue hundred, adding, that if he
would but change his countenance, and giue him no freendlie lookes
for a while, he should perceiue that Anselme would ad to the first offer,
other fiue hundred pounds. But Anselme was so far from being brought
to the kings lure with such fetches, that openlie to the kings face he told

him, that better it should be for his maiestie to receiue of him a small summe granted of him with a free and franke hart, so as he might helpe him eftsoones with more, than to take from him a great deale at once, without his good will, in such sort as if he were his bondman. For your grace (saith he) may haue me, and all that is mine, to serue your turne with freendlie beneuolence: but in the waie of seruitude and bondage you shall neither haue me nor mine. With which words the king was in maruellous choler, and therewith said in anger: "Well then, get thee home, take that which is thine to thy selfe that which I haue of mine owne I trust will suffice me." The archbishop beeing on his knees, rose herewith and departed, reioising in his mind that the king had refused his offer, whereby he was deliuered out of suspicion to haue bribed the king, and giuen him that monie in waie of reward for his preferment to the miter, as of malicious men would happilie haue beene construed. [Note: Matth. Paris.] Wherevpon beeing after laboured to double the summe he vtterlie refused, and determining rather to forsake the realme than to commit such an offense, made suit to the king for licence to go to Rome to fetch his pall of the pope. [Note: The king could not abide to heare the pope named.] The king hearing the pope named, waxed maruellous angrie: for they of Rome began alreadie to demand donations and contributions, more impudentlie than they were hitherto accustomed. And as it chanced, there was a schisme at that time in the church, by reason the emperor Henrie had placed a pope of his owne aduancing, (namely Wibteth archbishop of Rauenna) against pope Urban: for the emperor mainteined that it belonged to his office onlie to elect and as-signe what pope it pleased him.

King William therefore conceiued displeasure against Urban, who withstood the emperours pretense, and alledged by the like, that no arch-bishop or bishop within his realme should haue respect to the church of

Rome, nor to anie pope, with whome they had nothing to doo, either by waie of subiection, or otherwise; sith the popes wandered out of the steps which Peter trode, seeking after bribes, lucre, and worldlie honor. He said also that they could not reteine the power to lose and bind, which they sometime had, since they shewed themselues nothing at all to follow his most vertuous life and holie conuersation. He added furthermore, that for himselfe, sithens the conuersion of the realme to the christian faith, he had as great authoritie, franchises and liberties within the same, as the emperour had in his empire. And what hath the pope then to doo (quoth he) in the empire, or in my kingdome touching temporall liberties, whose dutie it is to be carefull for the soule of man, and to see that heresies spring not vp, which if the prelates of the prouince be not able to reforme, then might the pope doo it, either by himselfe or his legats. [Note: Eadmerus. The kings demand to Anselme.] Againe, by reason of the schisme, & for the displeasure that he bare pope Urban, he asked Anselme of which pope he would require his pall, sith he was so hastie to go to Rome for it. Wherto Anselme answered, that he would require it of pope Urban. Which words when the king had heard, he said, I haue not as yet admitted him pope: adding further that it was against the custome vsed either in his or his fathers time, that anie man within the realme of England should name or obeie anie man for pope, without the kings licence and consent, saieng moreouer, that if the said Anselme would seeke to take that prerogatiue and dignitie from him, it should be all one, as if he should go about to take awaie from him his crowne, and all other roiall dignitie. Wherevnto Anselme answered, that at Rochester (before he was consecrated bishop) he had declared his mind therein, and that beeing abbat of Bechellouin in Normandie, he had receiued Urban for pope; so that whatsoeuer chanced, he might reuolt from his obedience and subiection.

The king beeing the more kindled herewith, protested in plaine words, that Anselme could not keepe his faith and allegiance towards him, and his obedience also to the see of Rome, against his will and pleasure. [Note: A councell at Rockingham in Rutlandshire.] But (to conclude) this matter went so far in controuersie betwixt the king and the bishop, that a councell was called at Rockingham in Rutlandshire, and there in the church within the castell, the matter was earnestlie decided, and much adoo on euerie side, to haue constreined Anselme to renounce his opinion, but he would not. Wherfore it was then deuised, that if he would not agree to the kings pleasure, they would by and by see if they might by any meanes depriue him: but Anselme still held hard, and could not be feared by all these threats; and in like maner to iudge of an archbishops cause, the other bishops concluded that they had no authoritie.

Moreouer, while the matter was in consultation among the bishops, another of the kings councell that was a knight, came before Anselme in place where he sat almost alone, to looke for an answer by them from the king, which knight kneeling downe before the archbishop, spake these words vnto him: "Reuerend father, your humble children beseech your Grace not to haue your heart troubled with these things which you heare; but call to remembrance that blessed man Job, vanquishing the diuell on the dunghill, and reuenging Adam whome he had ouercome in paradise." Which words the archbishop considering with a freendlie countenance, perceiued that the minds of the people remained on his side, whereof both he and such as were about him, were right ioyfull and greatlie comforted, [Note: * If they be Gods people.] hauing hope, (according to the scripture) that the * voice of the people was the voice of God. When the king vnderstood all these things, he was maruelouslie disquieted in mind, and therefore perceiuing that the bishops and other of his councell had promised more than they could performe, he blamed them for it: vnto whom the bishop of Durham that was the cheefe dooer in this matter, framed this answer: "He spake so faintlie (quoth he) and so coldlie at the first, that he seemed not to haue any store of wit or wisdome."

Finallie, the matter was deferred vntill the next morning, and then the said bishop of Durham, alledging that they could not well ouercome him by arguments, so long as he grounded his opinion in such sort vpon the scripture, and the authoritie of Saint Peter; "The best way therefore (said he) shall be, to compell him by force, either to agree to the kings mind, or else to depriue him of his ring and staffe, and after banish him the realme." But the lords of the councell allowed not the bishops words herein. "Well (saith the king) and what other way will you thinke good, if this like you not: so long as I may liue, I will not surelie suffer any to be my peere within my realme: and if you knew his cause to be so good, why did you suffer me to commense this action against him: go your waies therefore, and take aduice togither, for by Gods face (for that was his oth) if you condemne him not at my will, I will reuenge myself vpon you." Neuerthelesse, when he was informed, that bicause he was an archbishop, they had no power to iudge or condemne him, though his cause prooued neuer so euill, which they could not perceiue[1] so to be; he told them yet they might at the leastwise renounce their obedience to him, and forsake his companie, which they said they might doo. "Then doo it (saith the king) with speed, that he may (when he shall see himselfe abandoned, and despised of all men) repent that he hath followed Urban, and neglected me his souereigne lord and maister. [Note: The king renounceth the archbishop for his subiect.] And that he may doo it the more safelie, first of all I depriue him of the suertie and allegiance which he may pretend to haue of me within all my dominions,

and from hencefoorth I will haue no affiance in him, nor take him for
an archbishop."

The bishops would faine haue persuaded Anselme to haue shewed
himselfe comformable to the kings pleasure, and therefore tooke paines
with him earnestlie in that behalfe, but all would not serue. He answered
indeed verie curteouslie, but his benefice he would not renounce, as
touching the name and office, though in exterior things he were neuer so much disquieted. The king perceiuing him to stand stiffe in his
opinion, said vnto his lords; "His words are euer contrarie to my mind,
and I will not take him for my freend, whosoeuer dooth fauour him. I
shall therefore require you that be peeres of my realme, to renounce all
the faith and freendship which you beare him, that he may see what
he hath gained by that allegiance, which (to the offending of my person) he obserueth to the apostolike see." Whereto the lords answered;
"As for vs, we were neuer his men, and therefore we cannot abiure
any fealtie which we neuer acknowledged. He is our archbishop, and
hath rule in matters perteining to christian religion within this land, for
which cause we that are christians may not refuse his authoritie whilest we remaine here on earth, bicause he is attainted with no blemish
of any heinous crime, which may constreine vs otherwise to doo." The
king refrained and dissembled his wrath, least he should prouoke them
to further displeasure by speaking against their reason.

[Note: The bishops driuen to their shifts how to shape an answer.]
The bishops were sore abashed hereat, and driuen to a shrewd pinch.
Now when, not long after, the king required to know of euerie of them
apart, whether they vtterlie renounced all manner of subiection and
obedience vnto Anselme without any condition intermitted, or else that
onelie which he did pretend by authoritie of the pope: the bishops making answer diuerslie herevnto, the king appointed those to sit downe

by him as faithfull subiects, who acknowledged that their renuntiation was absolutelie made, without intermitting of any condition: as for the other, who protested that they renounced their subiection and obedience vnto him onelie in that which he presumed vpon in the behalfe of the pope, he commanded them to go aside, and to remaine in a corner of the house to heare the sentence of their condemnation pronounced.

[Note: The meane to pacifie the king.] Wherefore being put in a maruellous feare, they withdrew themselues aside, but yet straightwaies they deuised a shift wherewith they had beene well acquainted before, as followeth. They presented to the king a great masse of monie to appease his wrath, and so thereby were restored to his fauour. [Note: The stiffenes of Anselme in withstanding the kings pleasure.] Anselme notwithstanding was obstinate in his opinion, so that in the end, the sentense touching this controuersie betwixt him and the king was respited till the octaues of Pentecost next ensuing. [Note: Matth. Paris.] All this was notified well inough to the pope, who vsed the matter with such moderation, that by secret aduertisements giuen, he tooke awaie from his brethren all rigorous waies of proceedings, saieng;   Dum furor in cursu est, currenti cede furori.

But yet the kings enmitie towards Anselme was openlie declared, and that cheefelie for the deniall of the monie which he demanded; but at length he got it, though not with any free heart or goodwill of the archbishop: insomuch that the king reputed him giltie of treason. Within a few daies after, Walter bishop of Alba, bringing to him his pall, verie wiselie reconciled the pope and the king. Notwithstanding all this, Anselme could not purchase the kings goodwill to his contentment, though he wiselie dissembled for the time; so that when the bishop of Alba should returne to Rome, he made sute for licence to go with him. Neuerthelesse, the king offered him, that if he would desist from his purpose, and sweare vpon the euangelists neither to go to Rome, nor to appeale in any cause to the popes court, he might and should liue in quietnesse free from all danger: [Note: Eadmerus.] but if he would not be so contented, he might and should depart at his perill, without hope to returne hither againe. "For surelie (saith he) if he go, I will seize the archbishoprike into mine owne hands, and receiue him no more for archbishop."

[Note: Fabian. Matth. Paris.] Anselme herewith departing from the court came to Canturburie, declaring openlie what had bin said vnto him, and immediatelie sought to flee out of the realme in the night, prouiding for himselfe a ship at Douer. But his purpose being reuealed to the king, one William Warlewast the kings seruant was sent after him, and finding him readie to depart, tooke from him all that he had, & gaue him a free pasport out of the land. [Note: Anselme comming to Rome complaineth of the king.] Anselme repairing to Rome, made vnto pope Urban a greeuous information against the king, declaring into what miserable state he had brought the Realme, and that for want of assistance in his suffragans it laie not in him to reforme the matter.

[Note: Ranelfe bishop of Chichester.] Indeed we find not that any of the bishops held with Anselme in the controuersie betwixt him and the king, Ranulph bishop of Chichester excepted, who both blamed the king and rebuked all such bishops as had refused to stand with Anselme, and fauoured the king in cases concerning the foresaid variance. Moreouer, the same bishop of Chichester withstood the king and his officers in taking fines of preests for the crime of fornication; by reason of which presumption, the king became sore offended with him: & found meanes to suspend many churches of his diocesse. Howbeit in the end, the bishop demeaned himselfe in suchwise, that he had his owne will, and his church doores were opened againe, which had beene stopped vp before with thornes. [Note: Fines of preests that had wiues as by some writers it seemed.] Besides this, the king was contented, that the said bishop should haue the fines of preests in crimes of fornication within his diocesse, and enioy many other priuileges in right of his church. [Note: Polydor.] But how beneficiall soeuer he was vnto the see of Chichester, true it is (as Polydor writeth) that he let out diuers abbeies, and the bishoprike of Winchester and Salisburie, with the archbishoprike of Canturburie vnto certeine persons that farmed the same at his hands for great summes of monie, in so much that (beside the said sees of Canturburie, Winchester, and Salisburie, which at the time of his death be kept in his hands) he also receiued the profits of eleuen abbeies which he had let out, or otherwise turned to his most aduantage[2].

[Note: Robert Losaunge. Ran. Higd. Wil. Malm.] Robert Losaunge, of some called Herbert, that sometime had bin abbat of Ramsey, and then bishop of Thetford by gift of a thousand pounds to the king (as before ye haue heard) repented him, for that he was inuested by the king, who after he had bewailed his offense, went to Rome, and did penance for the same in all points as the pope enioined him. Which being doone, he returned into England, remoouing yer long his see from Thetford to Norwich, where he founded a faire monasterie of his owne charges, and not of the churches goods (as some say) wherein is a doubt, considering he was first an abbat, and after a bishop.

[Note: Stephan Harding a moonke. Ran. Higd. Iacobus Philippus Berigonias.] About this time, by the meanes of Stephan Harding a Monke of Shireborne, an Englishman, the order of Cisteaux or white moonkes had his beginning within the countrie of Burgongne, as witnesneth Ranulph the moonke of Chester: but other writers (as Iacob. Philippus) say that this Stephan was the second abbat of that place, and that it was founded by one Robert abbat of Molmense, in the yeare of

Grace 1098. This order was after brought into England by one called Walter Espeke, who founded the first abbeie of that religion within this relme at Riuall, about the yeare of Grace 1131.

[Note: An. Reg. 13. 1100.] [Note: The kings lauish prodigalitie. Strange woonders. Wil. Malm.] But to returne againe to the king, who still continued in his wilfull couetousnesse, pulling from the rich and welthie, to waste and spend it out in all excesse, vaine riot, and gifts bestowed on such as had least deserued the same. And yet he was warned by manie strange woonders (as the common people did discant) to refraine from these euill doings: for the Thames did rise with such high springs and tides, that manie townes were drowned, and much hurt doone in places about London, and elsewhere. Diuerse rare things happened also at the same time, which I passe ouer. But the king hearing hereof, did nothing regard those which were so bold as to tell him that they were euident significations of some vengeance to follow therevpon. [Note: A dreame. Matth. West. Wil. Malm.] The king also himselfe on a night as he slept & dreamed, thought that the veines of his armes were broken, and that the blood issued out in great abundance. Likewise, he was told by Robert Fitz Hammon, that a moonke should dreame in his sleepe, how he saw the king gnaw the image of Christ crucified, with his teeth, and that as he was about to bite awaie the legs of the same image, Christ with his feet should spurne him downe to the ground, insomuch that as he lay on the earth, there came out of his mouth a flame of fire, and such abundance of smoke, that the aire was darkened therewith. But the king made a iest of these and the like tales; "He is a right moonke (saith he) and to haue a peece of monie, he dreameth such things, giue him therefore an hundred shillings, and bid him dreame of better fortune to our person." Neuerthelesse, the king was somewhat mooued herewith in the end, and doubted whether he should go into the new forest to hunt on Lammas day (as he had purposed) or no, bicause his freends councelled him not to trie the truth of dreames to his owne losse and hinderance. Wherevpon he forbare to go foorth before dinner, but when he had dined and made himselfe merrie with receiuing more drinke than commonlie he vsed to doo, abroad he got him into the forest with a small traine: [Note: Sir Walter Tirel.] amongst whom was one sir Walter Tirell a French knight, whom he had reteined in seruice with a large stipend.

This Sir Walter chanced to remaine with the king, when all the rest of the companie was dispersed here and there, as the maner in hunting is. Now as the sunne began to draw lowe, the king perceiuing an hart to come alongst by him, shot at the same, and with his arrow stroke him; but not greatlie hurting him, the beast ran awaie. The king, to mark which way the hart tooke, and the maner of his hurt, held vp his hand: betweene the sunne and his eies; who standing in that sort, out came another hart, at whom as sir Walter Tirell let driue an arrow, the same by glansing stroke the king into the brest, so that he neuer spake word, but breaking off so much of the arrow as appeared out of his bodie, he fell downe, and giuing onelie one grone, immediatlie died, without more noise or moouing. [Note: The king slaine.] Sir Walter running to him, and perceiuing no speech nor sense to remaine in him, straitwaies got to his horsse, and riding awaie, escaped and saued himselfe: for few there were that pursued him, euerie man being amazed at the chance, some departing one waie, and some another, euerie one for his owne aduantage and commoditie, as the time then serued. The dead bodie of the king was straight conueied to Winchester, and there buried the morrow after, which was the second day of August, the yere of our Lord 1100. [Note: Wil. Malm.] To this end came king William, after he had reigned almost 13 yeares, and liued 43 and somewhat more.

This prince, although euill reported of by writers for the couet-ous tasking of his subiects, and reteining of ecclesiasticall liuings in his hands; yet was he endued with manie noble and princelie qualities. He had good knowledge in feats of warre, and could well awaie with bodil-ie labour. In all his affaires he was circumspect; of his promise, trustie; of his word, stedfast; and in his wars no lesse diligent than fortunate. He gaue to the moonkes called Monachi de charitate in Southwarke, the great new church of S. Sauiour of Bermondsay, and also Bermondseie itselfe. He founded a goodlie hospitall in the citie of Yorke, called S. Leonards, for the sustentation and finding of the poore as well brethren as sisters. Towards souldiers and men of warre he was verie liberall, and to enrich them, he passed not for taking from farmers and husbandmen, what soeuer could be gotten. He was indeed of a prodigall nature, and therefore when in the begining of his reigne, doubting some troubles, he had assembled manie men of warre for his defense, there was noth-ing that they could aske which he would denie them, in somuch that his fathers treasures were soone consumed, by reason whereof he was put to his shifts to prouide more. For though substance wanted to shew his liberalitie, yet there failed not in him a mind still to be bountifull, sith continuall vse of giuing rewards, was in manner turned in him to a nature, so that to furnish himselfe with monie and necessaries, he was put to extremities vnbeseeming a king; and to bestow his beneuolence vpon some, he spared not to impouerish others. [Note: The liberall hart of king William.] For in such sort he was liberall, that therewith he was prodigall; and in such wise stout of courage, as proud withall; and in such maner seuere, as he seemed cruell and inexorable. But what meanes he vsed to make his best of benefices and spirituall liuings, par-tlie appeareth before.

[Note: Jewes.] In deed such was his condition, that who soeuer would

giue, might haue, & that oftentimes without respect, whether their sute
was reasonable and allowable or not, in somuch that it is said of him,
that being in Roan on a time, there came to him diuerse Jewes who in-
habited that citie, complaining to him, that diuerse of their nation had
renounced their Jewish religion, and were become christians: wherefore they besought him, that for a certeine summe of monie which they
offered to giue, it might please him to constreine them to abiure christi-
anitie, and turne to the Jewish law againe. He was contented to satisfie
their desires, and so receiuing the monie, called them before him, &
what with threats, and putting them otherwise in feare, he compelled
diuerse of them to forsake Christ, and returne to their old errors.

There was about the same time a yoong man a Jew, who by a vision appearing vnto him (as is said) was conuerted to the christian faith,
and being baptised, was named Stephan, bicause S. Stephan was the
man that had appeared to him in the vision, as by the same he was informed. The father of the yoong man being sore troubled, for that his
sonne was become a christian, and hearing what the king had doone
in such like matters, presented to him 60 markes of siluer, condittion-
ally that he should inforce his sonne to returne to his Jewish religion.
Herevpon was the yoong man brought before the king, vnto whom he
said; "Sirra, thy father here complaineth that without his licence thou
art become a christian: if this be true, I command thee to returne againe
to the religion of thy nation, without anie more adoo". To whom the
yoongman answered, "Your grace (as I gesse) dooth but iest." Wherewith the king being mooued said, "What thou dunghill knaue, should
I iest with thee? Get thee hence quicklie, and fulfill my commandement, or by S. Lukes face I shall cause thine eies to be plucked out of
thine head." [Note: An answer of a good Jew.] The yoongman nothing
abashed hereat, with a constant voice answered "Trulie I will not doo

it, but know for certeine, that if you were a good christian, you would neuer haue vttered anie such words, for it is the part of a christian to reduce them againe to Christ which be departed from him; & not to separate them from him, which are ioined to him by faith." The king herewith confounded, commanded the Jew to auant & get him out of his sight. But his father perceiuing that the king could not persuade his sonne to forsake the christian faith, required to haue his monie againe. To whom the king said, he had doone so much as he promised to doo, that was, to persuade him so far as he might. [Note: A prettie diuision.] At length, when he would haue had the king to haue dealt further in the matter, the king (to stop his mouth) tendered backe to him the one halfe of his monie, & reteined the other to himselfe.

[Note: King William suspected of infidelitie.] Moreouer, to increase the suspicion which men had of his infidelitie, it is written, that he caused a disputation to be kept betwixt the Jewes & the christians, promising that if the Jewes ouercame the christians in argument, he would be a Jew: but the Jewes being ouercome, and receiuing the foile, would not confess their errors, but alledged, that by factions (and not by reason) they were put to the worse. Howbeit, what opinion soeuer he had of the Jewes faith, it appeereth by writers that he doubted in manie points of the religion then in credit. [Note: Eadmerus.] For he sticked not to protest openlie, that he beleeued no saint could profit anie man in the Lords sight, and therefore neither would he nor anie other that was wise (as he affirmed) make intercession, either to Peter, or to anie other for helpe. [Note: Praieng to saincts.]

[Note: His stature. Whereof he tooke his surname Rufus.] He was of stature not so tall as the common sort of men, red of haire, whereof he tooke his surname Rufus, somwhat big of bellie, and not readie of toong, speciallie in his anger, for then his vtterance was so hindered, that he could scarselie shew the conceits of his mind: he died without issue, and vsed concubines all the daies of his life. I find that in apparell he loued to be gaie and gorgeous, & could not abide to haue anie thing (for his wearing) esteemed at a small valure. [Note: Wil. Malm.] Wherevpon it came to passe on a morning, when he should pull on a new paire of hose, he asked the groome of his chamber that brought them to him what they cost? Three shillings saith he; "Why thou hooreson (said the king) dooth a paire of hose of three shillings price become a king to weare? Go thy waies, and fetch me a paire that shall cost a marke of siluer." The groome went, and brought him another paire, for the which he paid scarselie so much as for the first. But when the king asked what they stood him in, he told him they cost a marke: and then was he well satisfied, and said; "Yea marie, these are more fit for a king to weare, and so drew them vpon his legs."

In this kings daies John bishop of Welles ioined the monasterie of Bath vnto his see, and repairing the same monasterie, began to inhabit there in the yeere 1094. [Note: Couentrie church ioined to the see of Chester.] The Church of Couentrie was in like sort ioined vnto the see of Chester by Robert bishop of that diocesse. Woolstan bishop of Worcester died about the same time, and Anselme hauing purchased bulles of pope Paschall, wherein was conteined an admonition vnto king William to desist from his greeuous oppressing of the church, and to amend his former dooings, was now on his returne towards England, and by the waie heard of the kings death. Hugh earle of Chester in this kings daies builded the abbeie of Chester, and procured Anselme (afterwards archbishop of Canturburie) to come ouer from Normandie, that he might erect the same abbeie, and place such religious persons as were necessarie and conuenient for so good a foundation.

Long it was yer Anselme would come ouer, bicause he doubted to be had in suspicion of an ambitious desire in seeking to be made arch-bishop of Canturburie. For it was talked that if he went ouer into England, he should surelie be elected before he returned into Normandie. But at length so it chanced, that the aforesaid Hugh earle of Chester fell sicke, and despairing of life, sent with all speed to Anselme, requiring him most instantlie to come ouer to him lieng in extremitie of sickness; adding, that if he hasted not the sooner, it would be too late, whereof he would after repent him. Then Anselme, for that he might not faile his freend in such necessitie, came ouer, and gaue order to the abbeie, according as it seemed best to him for the establishment of religion there.

thus farre William Rufus.

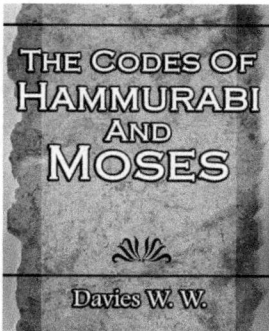

The Codes Of Hammurabi And Moses
W. W. Davies

QTY

The discovery of the Hammurabi Code is one of the greatest achievements of archaeology, and is of paramount interest, not only to the student of the Bible, but also to all those interested in ancient history...

Religion   **ISBN:** *1-59462-338-4*   **Pages:132**
MSRP $12.95

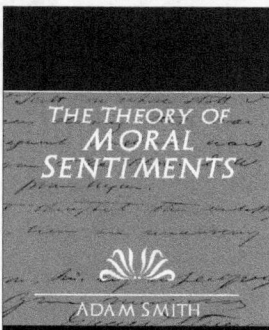

The Theory of Moral Sentiments
Adam Smith

QTY

This work from 1749. contains original theories of conscience amd moral judgment and it is the foundation for systemof morals.

Philosophy   **ISBN:** *1-59462-777-0*   **Pages:536**
MSRP $19.95

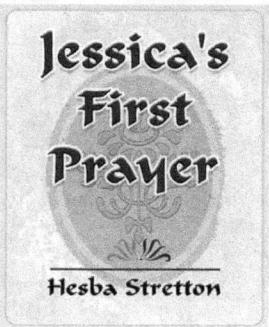

Jessica's First Prayer
Hesba Stretton

QTY

In a screened and secluded corner of one of the many railway-bridges which span the streets of London there could be seen a few years ago, from five o'clock every morning until half past eight, a tidily set-out coffee-stall, consisting of a trestle and board, upon which stood two large tin cans, with a small fire of charcoal burning under each so as to keep the coffee boiling during the early hours of the morning when the work-people were thronging into the city on their way to their daily toil...

Pages:84

Childrens   **ISBN:** *1-59462-373-2*   *MSRP $9.95*

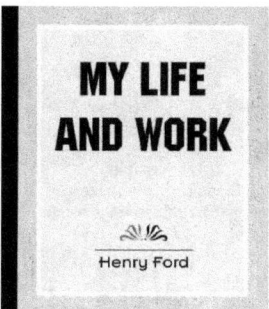

My Life and Work
Henry Ford

QTY

Henry Ford revolutionized the world with his implementation of mass production for the Model T automobile. Gain valuable business insight into his life and work with his own auto-biography... "We have only started on our development of our country we have not as yet, with all our talk of wonderful progress, done more than scratch the surface. The progress has been wonderful enough but..."

Pages:300

Biographies/ **ISBN:** *1-59462-198-5*   *MSRP $21.95*

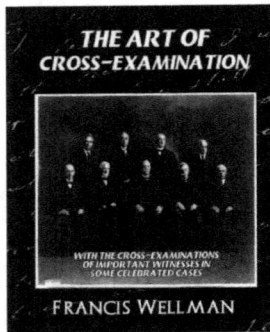

The Art of Cross-Examination
Francis Wellman

QTY

I presume it is the experience of every author, after his first book is published upon an important subject, to be almost overwhelmed with a wealth of ideas and illustrations which could readily have been included in his book, and which to his own mind, at least, seem to make a second edition inevitable. Such certainly was the case with me; and when the first edition had reached its sixth impression in five months, I rejoiced to learn that it seemed to my publishers that the book had met with a sufficiently favorable reception to justify a second and considerably enlarged edition. ..

Reference   **ISBN: *1-59462-647-2***

Pages:412
MSRP $19.95

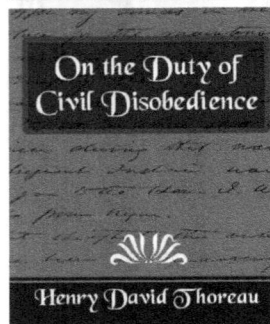

On the Duty of Civil Disobedience
Henry David Thoreau

QTY

Thoreau wrote his famous essay, On the Duty of Civil Disobedience, as a protest against an unjust but popular war and the immoral but popular institution of slave-owning. He did more than write—he declined to pay his taxes, and was hauled off to gaol in consequence. Who can say how much this refusal of his hastened the end of the war and of slavery ?

Law   **ISBN: *1-59462-747-9***

Pages:48
MSRP $7.45

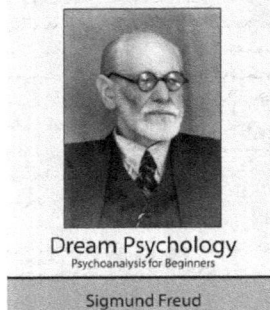

Dream Psychology Psychoanalysis for Beginners
Sigmund Freud

QTY

Sigmund Freud, born Sigismund Schlomo Freud (May 6, 1856 - September 23, 1939), was a Jewish-Austrian neurologist and psychiatrist who co-founded the psychoanalytic school of psychology. Freud is best known for his theories of the unconscious mind, especially involving the mechanism of repression; his redefinition of sexual desire as mobile and directed towards a wide variety of objects; and his therapeutic techniques, especially his understanding of transference in the therapeutic relationship and the presumed value of dreams as sources of insight into unconscious desires.

Psychology   **ISBN: *1-59462-905-6***

Pages:196
MSRP $15.45

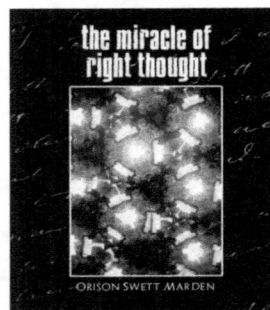

The Miracle of Right Thought
Orison Swett Marden

QTY

Believe with all of your heart that you will do what you were made to do. When the mind has once formed the habit of holding cheerful, happy, prosperous pictures, it will not be easy to form the opposite habit. It does not matter how improbable or how far away this realization may see, or how dark the prospects may be, if we visualize them as best we can, as vividly as possible, hold tenaciously to them and vigorously struggle to attain them, they will gradually become actualized, realized in the life. But a desire, a longing without endeavor, a yearning abandoned or held indifferently will vanish without realization.

Self Help   **ISBN: *1-59462-644-8***

Pages:360
MSRP $25.45

The Rosicrucian Cosmo-Conception Mystic Christianity by *Max Heindel*   ISBN: *1-59462-188-8*   **$38.95**
The Rosicrucian Cosmo-conception is not dogmatic, neither does it appeal to any other authority than the reason of the student. It is: not controversial, but is: sent forth in the, hope that it may help to clear.,.   *New Age/Religion Pages 646*

Abandonment To Divine Providence by *Jean-Pierre de Caussade*   ISBN: *1-59462-228-0*   **$25.95**
"The Rev. Jean Pierre de Caussade was one of the most remarkable spiritual writers of the Society of Jesus in France in the 18th Century. His death took place at Toulouse in 1751. His works have gone through many editions and have been republished...   *Inspirational/Religion Pages 400*

Mental Chemistry by *Charles Haanel*   ISBN: *1-59462-192-6*   **$23.95**
Mental Chemistry allows the change of material conditions by combining and appropriately utilizing the power of the mind. Much like applied chemistry creates something new and unique out of careful combinations of chemicals the mastery of mental chemistry...   *New Age Pages 354*

The Letters of Robert Browning and Elizabeth Barret Barrett 1845-1846 vol II   ISBN: *1-59462-193-4*   **$35.95**
by *Robert Browning* and *Elizabeth Barrett*   *Biographies Pages 596*

Gleanings In Genesis (volume I) by *Arthur W. Pink*   ISBN: *1-59462-130-6*   **$27.45**
Appropriately has Genesis been termed "the seed plot of the Bible" for in it we have, in germ form, almost all of the great doctrines which are afterwards fully developed in the books of Scripture which follow...   *Religion/Inspirational Pages 420*

The Master Key by *L. W. de Laurence*   ISBN: *1-59462-001-6*   **$30.95**
In no branch of human knowledge has there been a more lively increase of the spirit of research during the past few years than in the study of Psychology, Concentration and Mental Discipline. The requests for authentic lessons in Thought Control, Mental Discipline and...   *New Age/Business Pages 422*

The Lesser Key Of Solomon Goetia by *L. W. de Laurence*   ISBN: *1-59462-092-X*   **$9.95**
This translation of the first book of the "Lernegton" which is now for the first time made accessible to students of Talismanic Magic was done, after careful collation and edition, from numerous Ancient Manuscripts in Hebrew, Latin, and French...   *New Age/Occult Pages 92*

Rubaiyat Of Omar Khayyam by *Edward Fitzgerald*   ISBN:*1-59462-332-5*   **$13.95**
Edward Fitzgerald, whom the world has already learned, in spite of his own efforts to remain within the shadow of anonymity, to look upon as one of the rarest poets of the century, was born at Bredfield, in Suffolk, on the 31st of March, 1809. He was the third son of John Purcell...   *Music Pages 172*

Ancient Law by *Henry Maine*   ISBN: *1-59462-128-4*   **$29.95**
The chief object of the following pages is to indicate some of the earliest ideas of mankind, as they are reflected in Ancient Law, and to point out the relation of those ideas to modern thought.   *Religiom/History Pages 452*

Far-Away Stories by *William J. Locke*   ISBN: *1-59462-129-2*   **$19.45**
"Good wine needs no bush, but a collection of mixed vintages does. And this book is just such a collection. Some of the stories I do not want to remain buried for ever in the museum files of dead magazine-numbers an author's not unpardonable vanity..."   *Fiction Pages 272*

Life of David Crockett by *David Crockett*   ISBN: *1-59462-250-7*   **$27.45**
"Colonel David Crockett was one of the most remarkable men of the times in which he lived. Born in humble life, but gifted with a strong will, an indomitable courage, and unremitting perseverance...   *Biographies/New Age Pages 424*

Lip-Reading by *Edward Nitchie*   ISBN: *1-59462-206-X*   **$25.95**
Edward B. Nitchie, founder of the New York School for the Hard of Hearing, now the Nitchie School of Lip-Reading, Inc, wrote "LIP-READING Principles and Practice". The development and perfecting of this meritorious work on lip-reading was an undertaking...   *How-to Pages 400*

A Handbook of Suggestive Therapeutics, Applied Hypnotism, Psychic Science   ISBN: *1-59462-214-0*   **$24.95**
by *Henry Munro*   *Health/New Age/Health/Self-help Pages 376*

A Doll's House: and Two Other Plays by *Henrik Ibsen*   ISBN: *1-59462-112-8*   **$19.95**
Henrik Ibsen created this classic when in revolutionary 1848 Rome. Introducing some striking concepts in playwriting for the realist genre, this play has been studied the world over.   *Fiction/Classics/Plays 308*

The Light of Asia by *sir Edwin Arnold*   ISBN: *1-59462-204-3*   **$13.95**
In this poetic masterpiece, Edwin Arnold describes the life and teachings of Buddha. The man who was to become known as Buddha to the world was born as Prince Gautama of India but he rejected the worldly riches and abandoned the reigns of power when... Religion/History/Biographies Pages 170

The Complete Works of Guy de Maupassant by *Guy de Maupassant*   ISBN: *1-59462-157-8*   **$16.95**
"For days and days, nights and nights, I had dreamed of that first kiss which was to consecrate our engagement, and I knew not on what spot I should put my lips..."   *Fiction/Classics Pages 240*

The Art of Cross-Examination by *Francis L. Wellman*   ISBN: *1-59462-309-0*   **$26.95**
Written by a renowned trial lawyer, Wellman imparts his experience and uses case studies to explain how to use psychology to extract desired information through questioning.   *How-to/Science/Reference Pages 408*

Answered or Unanswered? by *Louisa Vaughan*   ISBN: *1-59462-248-5*   **$10.95**
Miracles of Faith in China   *Religion Pages 112*

The Edinburgh Lectures on Mental Science (1909) by *Thomas*   ISBN: *1-59462-008-3*   **$11.95**
This book contains the substance of a course of lectures recently given by the writer in the Queen Street Hail, Edinburgh. Its purpose is to indicate the Natural Principles governing the relation between Mental Action and Material Conditions...   *New Age/Psychology Pages 148*

Ayesha by *H. Rider Haggard*   ISBN: *1-59462-301-5*   **$24.95**
Verily and indeed it is the unexpected that happens! Probably if there was one person upon the earth from whom the Editor of this, and of a certain previous history, did not expect to hear again...   *Classics Pages 380*

Ayala's Angel by *Anthony Trollope*   ISBN: *1-59462-352-X*   **$29.95**
The two girls were both pretty, but Lucy who was twenty-one who supposed to be simple and comparatively unattractive, whereas Ayala was credited, as her Bombwhat romantic name might show, with poetic charm and a taste for romance. Ayala when her father died was nineteen... Fiction Pages 484

The American Commonwealth by *James Bryce*   ISBN: *1-59462-286-8*   **$34.45**
An interpretation of American democratic political theory. It examines political mechanics and society from the perspective of Scotsman James Bryce   *Politics Pages 572*

Stories of the Pilgrims by *Margaret P. Pumphrey*   ISBN: *1-59462-116-0*   **$17.95**
This book explores pilgrims religious oppression in England as well as their escape to Holland and eventual crossing to America on the Mayflower, and their early days in New England...   *History Pages 268*

QTY

The Fasting Cure *by Sinclair Upton*
ISBN: *1-59462-222-1* **$13.95**
In the Cosmopolitan Magazine for May, 1910, and in the Contemporary Review (London) for April, 1910, I published an article dealing with my experiences in fasting. I have written a great many magazine articles, but never one which attracted so much attention... New Age/Self Help/Health Pages 164

Hebrew Astrology *by Sepharial*
ISBN: *1-59462-308-2* **$13.45**
In these days of advanced thinking it is a matter of common observation that we have left many of the old landmarks behind and that we are now pressing forward to greater heights and to a wider horizon than that which represented the mind-content of our progenitors... Astrology Pages 144

Thought Vibration or The Law of Attraction in the Thought World
ISBN: *1-59462-127-6* **$12.95**
by William Walker Atkinson
Psychology/Religion Pages 144

Optimism *by Helen Keller*
ISBN: *1-59462-108-X* **$15.95**
Helen Keller was blind, deaf, and mute since 19 months old, yet famously learned how to overcome these handicaps, communicate with the world, and spread her lectures promoting optimism. An inspiring read for everyone... Biographies/Inspirational Pages 84

Sara Crewe *by Frances Burnett*
ISBN: *1-59462-360-0* **$9.45**
In the first place, Miss Minchin lived in London. Her home was a large, dull, tall one, in a large, dull square, where all the houses were alike, and all the sparrows were alike, and where all the door-knockers made the same heavy sound... Childrens/Classic Pages 88

The Autobiography of Benjamin Franklin *by Benjamin Franklin*
ISBN: *1-59462-135-7* **$24.95**
The Autobiography of Benjamin Franklin has probably been more extensively read than any other American historical work, and no other book of its kind has had such ups and downs of fortune. Franklin lived for many years in England, where he was agent... Biographies/History Pages 332

Name	
Email	
Telephone	
Address	
City, State ZIP	

☐ **Credit Card**   ☐ **Check / Money Order**

Credit Card Number	
Expiration Date	
Signature	

Please Mail to: *Book Jungle*
PO Box 2226
Champaign, IL 61825
or Fax to: *630-214-0564*

ORDERING INFORMATION
web: *www.bookjungle.com*
email: *sales@bookjungle.com*
fax: *630-214-0564*
mail: *Book Jungle PO Box 2226 Champaign, IL 61825*
or PayPal *to sales@bookjungle.com*

Please contact us for bulk discounts

DIRECT-ORDER TERMS

**20% Discount if You Order
Two or More Books**
Free Domestic Shipping!
Accepted: Master Card, Visa,
Discover, American Express